Sing Gently

Eric Whitacre

Piano Quintet

ISBN 978-1-70511-391-2

HAL•LEONARD®

www.ericwhitacre.com
www.halleonard.com

Contact us:
Hal Leonard
7777 West Bluemound Road
Milwaukee, WI 53213
Email: info@halleonard.com

In Europe, contact:
Hal Leonard Europe Limited
42 Wigmore Street
Marylebone, London, W1U 2RN
Email: info@halleonardeurope.com

In Australia, contact:
Hal Leonard Australia Pty. Ltd.
4 Lentara Court
Cheltenham, Victoria, 3192 Australia
Email: info@halleonard.com.au

SING GENTLY

Music from Virtual Choir 6
for piano and string quartet

Eric Whitacre

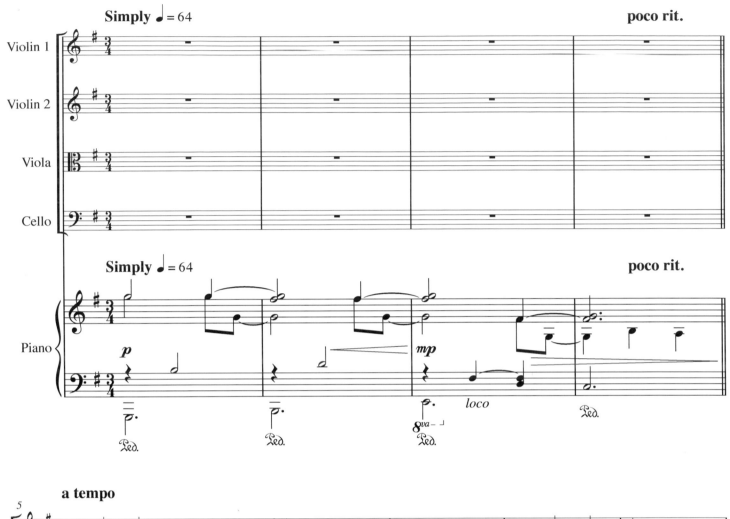

SING GENTLY

Music from Virtual Choir 6
for piano and string quartet

Violin 1

Eric Whitacre

SING GENTLY

Music from Virtual Choir 6
for piano and string quartet

Eric Whitacre

Violin 2

SING GENTLY

Music from Virtual Choir 6
for piano and string quartet

Viola

Eric Whitacre

SING GENTLY

Music from Virtual Choir 6
for piano and string quartet

Eric Whitacre

Cello

6

Los Angeles, June, 2020

NOTES FROM THE COMPOSER

In March of 2020, as the COVID-19 crisis began to unfold around the world, it became clear that this moment in history was going to be remembered as one of great suffering for many people, as well as a time of growing division and dissent. It seemed that as the global community began to isolate physically from one another, the same kind of isolation was happening on a social level, that the very fabric of society was tearing at the seams.

In that spirit I wrote the music and words to *Sing Gently* with the hope that it might give some small measure of comfort for those who need it, and that it might suggest a way of living with one another that is compassionate, gentle, and kind.

Sing Gently received its premiere online on July 19th, 2020, performed by the 17,572 singers of Virtual Choir 6.

~Eric Whitacre

May we sing together,
Always,
May our voice be soft,
May our singing be music for others,
And may it keep others aloft.

Sing gently, always,
Sing gently as one.

May we stand together,
Always,
May our voice be strong,
May we hear the singing, always,
And may we always sing along.

Sing gently, always,
Sing gently as one.

ABOUT THE COMPOSER

Grammy Award-winning composer and conductor, **Eric Whitacre**, is among today's most popular musicians. His works are programmed worldwide and his Virtual Choirs have united singers from more than 145 countries over the last decade. Born in Nevada in 1970, Eric is a graduate of the prestigious Juilliard School of Music (New York) and served two terms as Artist in Residence with the Los Angeles Master Chorale following five years as Composer in Residence at Cambridge University (UK).

His compositions have been widely recorded and his debut album as a conductor on *Universal*, *Light and Gold*, went straight to the top of the charts. As a guest conductor he has drawn capacity audiences to concerts with many of the world's leading orchestras and choirs in venues from Carnegie Hall (New York) to the Royal Albert Hall (London). Insatiably curious, Eric has worked with legendary Hollywood composer Hans Zimmer, as well as British pop icons Laura Mvula, Imogen Heap and Annie Lennox.

In 2018 his composition, *Deep Field*, became the foundation for a pioneering collaboration with NASA, STScI, Music Productions and film-makers 59 Productions. His long-form work *The Sacred Veil*, a profound meditation on love, life and loss, was premiered by the Los Angeles Master Chorale and released on Signum Records in 2020. His collaboration with Spitfire Audio resulted in a trail-blazing vocal sample library, became an instant best-seller and is used by composers the world-over. A charismatic speaker, Eric Whitacre has given keynote addresses for TED, Apple, Google, the United Nations Speaker's Program, in education and for global institutions.